EXPLORING THE WORLD

LA SALLE

*La Salle and the
Mississippi River*

BY ANN HEINRICHS

Content Adviser: Maria Concepcion, M.S., Latin American and Caribbean Studies,
New York University

Social Science Adviser: Professor Sherry L. Field, Department of Curriculum and Instruction,
College of Education, The University of Texas at Austin

Reading Adviser: Dr. Linda D. Labbo, Department of Reading Education,
College of Education, The University of Georgia

COMPASS POINT BOOKS
MINNEAPOLIS, MINNESOTA

Compass Point Books
3722 West 50th Street, #115
Minneapolis, MN 55410

Visit Compass Point Books on the Internet at *www.compasspointbooks.com* or
e-mail your request to *custserv@compasspointbooks.com*

Photographs ©: North Wind Picture Archives, cover, back cover (background), 1, 2 (background), 9,
20, 21, 22, 25, 29, 36, 39; Richard Hamilton Smith, 5; Bettmann/Corbis, 6; Franz-Marc Frei/Corbis,
7; Stock Montage, 8, 16, 30, 32, 46-47 (background); Leonard de Selva/Corbis, 10; Dave G.
Houser/Corbis, 11; Thomas Kitchin/Tom Stack & Associates, 12; Nathan Benn/Corbis, 13; Hulton
Getty/Archive Photos, 14, 24; Jeff Foott/Tom Stack & Associates, 15; Robert Estall/Corbis, 18;
Giraudon/Art Resource, N.Y., 23; William A. Bake/Corbis, 26; Paul Mellon Collection, National
Gallery of Art, Washington, 27; N. Carter/North Wind Picture Archives, 28; Historical Picture
Archive/Corbis, 31; Clint Farlinger/Visuals Unlimited, 33; Archivo Iconografico, S. A./Corbis, 34;
Réunion des Musées Nationaux/Art Resource, N.Y., 35; Texas Historical Commission, 37 (both);
David Muench/Corbis, 40; Paul Almasy/Corbis, 41.

Editors: E. Russell Primm, Emily J. Dolbear, and Melissa McDaniel
Photo Researchers: Svetlana Zhurkina and Jo Miller
Photo Selector: Catherine Neitge
Designer: Design Lab
Cartographer: XNR Productions, Inc.

Library of Congress Cataloging-in-Publication Data
Heinrichs, Ann.
    La Salle : La Salle and the Mississippi River / by Ann Heinrichs.
      p. cm. — (Exploring the world)
    Includes bibliographical references and index.
    Summary: A biography of the seventeenth-century French explorer who was the first European
to travel the entire length of the Mississippi River, claiming for France not only that river, but also
all the land whose waters fed into it.
    ISBN 0-7565-0178-4
    1. La Salle, Robert Cavelier, sieur de, 1643–1687—Juvenile literature. 2. Explorers—
Mississippi River Valley—Biography—Juvenile literature. 3. Explorers—France—Biography—
Juvenile literature. 4. Mississippi River Valley—Discovery and exploration—French—Juvenile literature. 5. Mississippi River Valley—History—To 1803—Juvenile literature. 6. Canada—History—To
1763 (New France)—Juvenile literature. [1. La Salle, Robert Cavelier, sieur de, 1643-1687. 2.
Explorers. 3. Mississippi River—Discovery and exploration.] I. Title. II. Series.
    F352 .H47 2002
    977'.01'092—dc21   2001004729

Table of Contents

An Empire of His Own

In 1682, French explorer René-Robert Cavelier, Sieur de La Salle, stood at the mouth of the Mississippi River, looking out over the blue waters of the Gulf of Mexico. Starting from Canada, La Salle had explored the Mississippi all the way south to its end. He was the first European to do that. Now La Salle claimed all the land whose waters flowed into that mighty river. This meant that more than half of what is now the United States became the property of France. La Salle named the region *Louisiana* after his king, Louis the Fourteenth (XIV) of France.

Today, Louisiana is just a medium-sized Southern state. But in 1682, when La Salle claimed it, Louisiana was the very heart of North America. It stretched from the Allegheny Mountains in the east, to the Rocky Mountains in the west. Louisiana was a land of lush forests, tall mountains, rich prairies, and thousands of rivers and streams.

When he claimed Louisiana, La Salle added a huge area to France's property. But he also

The Mississippi River

René-Robert Cavelier, Sieur de La Salle, takes possession of Louisiana.

had his own goals in mind. He planned to set up a **colony** in Louisiana that would be his very own **empire**. Sadly, that desire would drive the bold explorer to a disgraceful end.

The Early Years

René-Robert Cavelier was born in Rouen in northern France in 1643. Houses, shops, and busy market stalls lined Rouen's narrow, winding streets. Over them loomed the huge Cathedral of Notre-Dame. Every day its bells echoed far across the countryside.

When Robert was growing up, Rouen was an important port on the Seine River. Ships sailed from the French capital

The cathedral at Rouen

Rouen was an important port on the Seine.

of Paris, past Rouen, to the port of Le Havre. There they entered the English Channel and headed out into the Atlantic Ocean. Some were trading ships, bound for faraway lands. Others sailed on voyages of exploration. For a young man in Rouen, the ships were a daily reminder of exciting worlds across the sea.

The Caveliers were a rich family. Robert's father was a trader who owned large **estates** of rolling hills and farmland. One estate was called La Salle. In those days, a son often took the name of a family estate. In Robert's case, he was called Sieur de La Salle, or "Gentleman of La Salle."

Robert's older brother, Jean, became a priest. Robert himself went to a school run by priests. As a student, he was very good in mathematics. He also had a flair for the sciences.

When Robert was seventeen, he took vows as a **novice**. This was a first step on the way to becoming a priest. During his six years as a novice, Robert taught boys in the school. As time went on, though, he became restless. He decided that the quiet life of a priest was not for him. He needed adventure! So Robert gave up the idea of being a priest and set out to make his fortune in the world.

In France at that time, a young man who took religious vows could not **inherit** his family's property. Even though

Roman Catholic priests could not inherit family property.

Robert had decided not to become a priest, he had already taken his first vows. By French law, he could never inherit his family's land. With no future for him at home, Robert set his sights across the Atlantic Ocean.

A chapel in France

Learning the Ways of the Wilderness

At the age of twenty-three, the young Sieur de La Salle boarded a ship for New France. That was France's new colony in North America. It covered what is now eastern Canada and the Great Lakes region. Robert's brother, Jean, was already

This seminary in Montreal was built in 1683.

there. His group of priests owned the land in Montreal, the capital of New France. Montreal stood on an island in the St. Lawrence River.

After crossing the Atlantic, La Salle's ship entered the mouth of the St. Lawrence River. It sailed up the river to the island of Montreal. Along the waterfront, La Salle saw a row of small houses where settlers lived.

The priests gave a lot of land to settlers. They thought the settlements would protect them from attacks by local Iroquois Indians. With his brother's help, La Salle was given a huge piece of land at the south-

Dense forests line the St. Lawrence River.

An Iroquois dances outside a reconstructed traditional longhouse.

west end of Montreal Island. Today that spot is the city of Lachine. Now La Salle himself had plenty of land to rent out to other settlers.

After a visit with his brother, La Salle headed off into the forest. Thick woods of pine and oak covered this entire region of North America. It was the homeland of the Iroquois Confederacy, an Indian nation made up of five tribes.

As La Salle made his way through the forest, he could hear the distant roar of **rapids** on the St. Lawrence River. They are now called the Lachine

Fur traders traveled in birch–bark canoes.

Rapids. When he reached the southwest end of the island, he began to clear the forest and plan a village. First he chose a place to build his own home. Then he marked out sections of land for other settlers. He charged each settler a yearly fee in money and chickens.

Trading furs was the best way to make a living in New France. Being a fur trader meant making friends with the Indians, who hunted and trapped animals. La Salle settled into his new home and began studying the local Indian languages. If he wanted to trade with them, he had to talk with them. He built a trading post and, in time, grew rich from trading furs. The wealthier he got, the greedier he became. He secretly hoped to take over the entire fur trade in New France.

La Salle was also dreaming of an even bigger adventure. He wanted to find a

La Salle hoped to find a passage to the Gulf of California.

southwest passage, a water route that would lead to the Vermilion Sea. Today, that sea is known as the Gulf of California, which opens into the Pacific Ocean. La Salle knew that China lay across the Pacific. Trading in silk and other valuable goods from China could bring amazing riches.

In 1669, La Salle set out by canoe to try to find the southwest passage. With him were crew members, some Indian guides, and a few priests. If they met Indians along the way, the priests would try to convince them to become Christians.

La Salle

La Salle and his men traveled up the St. Lawrence River and across Lake Ontario. According to one member of his crew, La Salle "was undertaking this journey almost in a daze, more or less not knowing where he was going." One by one, his men left him. When they got back to La Salle's

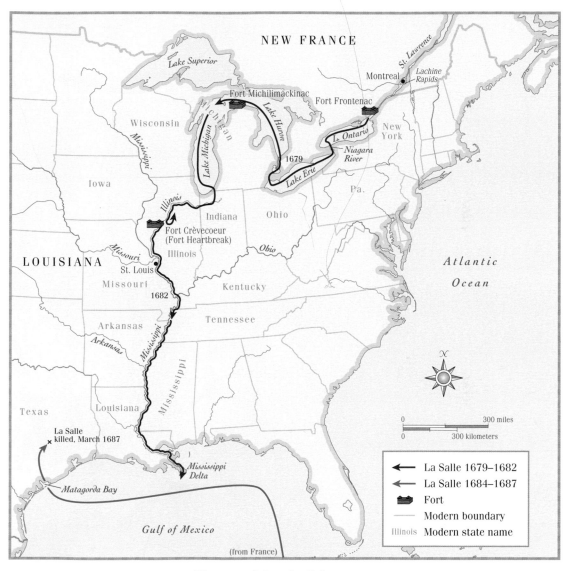

A map of La Salle's voyages

La Salle and his men canoed through Lake Ontario.

settlement, they named it *La Chine*—French for "China." It was their way of making fun of La Salle's wild dreams.

No one is sure how far La Salle explored or what he discovered during the next two years. He may have reached Lake Michigan and explored the Illinois River. In any case, he realized that no river flowed from the Great Lakes into the Vermilion Sea.

Back in Montreal, La Salle heard about another voyage. In 1673, the French-Canadian Louis Jolliet had explored the Mississippi River—the "Big River," as the Indians called it. With Jacques Marquette, a French missionary, Jolliet had gone down the river as far as the Arkansas River. He didn't make it all the way to the river's mouth. However, he was sure that the Mississippi emptied into the Gulf of Mexico.

Jolliet's voyage made La Salle a bit jealous, but it also gave him an idea. If he traveled down the river to the Gulf of Mexico, he might be able to start a colony of his own. He thought about how large his fur trade would be then. It would be an empire!

Now La Salle had more reason than ever to build up his fur-trading business. The money would help pay for his trip. He talked about his idea with Count Louis de Frontenac, the governor of New France. Frontenac liked the idea of controlling the entire

Mississippi River Valley. With the help of Frontenac, La Salle pushed other traders out of the way, taking over the areas they had controlled. Then, in 1677, La Salle sailed back to France. He would have to sell King Louis on the idea of his grand trip.

Louis Jolliet and Father Jacques Marquette explored the Mississippi River in 1673.

Count Louis de Frontenac

Off to a Rough Start

King Louis liked La Salle's plan and awarded him even more land in New France. He also agreed to La Salle's plan to explore the Mississippi to its mouth. La Salle was to set up forts along the way.

The biggest problem for La

A bust of King Louis XIV is in Quebec.

Salle was that he would have to pay for the trip himself. He needed money—a lot of money. He borrowed some in France, and he borrowed more in Montreal. Then he was able to build the *Griffin*, a 45-ton ship with five huge cannons built into the sides. One

The construction of the Griffin *is depicted in this engraving that appeared in a French book in 1711.*

of his men was a daring Italian named Henri de Tonty (Tonti). The two became close friends. At last, in 1679, La Salle launched the *Griffin* on the Niagara River, beyond its now famous falls.

The *Griffin* crossed Lake Erie and sailed up through Lake Huron. On the shores of Lake Michigan, La Salle shocked everyone. The *Griffin* was a gunboat, meant to protect the crew. But La Salle had something else in mind. He loaded the *Griffin* with furs and sent it back to Montreal. The furs were supposed to pay off his debts. Then the *Griffin* was to sail back and join La Salle. As it turned out, the *Griffin* was never seen again.

After the *Griffin* left, La Salle pushed on by canoe. When he reached the Illinois River, he went upstream and built Fort Crèvecoeur (Fort Heartbreak) at present-day Peoria, Illinois. Winter was coming, and the men set up a camp while La Salle waited for the *Griffin* to return.

La Salle

Finally, he could wait no longer. Leaving Tonty in charge of the fort, La Salle headed back to Montreal by canoe and on foot—more than 1,000 miles (1,610 kilometers)! He set off into the wilderness with four Frenchmen and an Indian guide. They left in March, as the ice and snow began to thaw. The Iroquois had taught La Salle how to travel long distances on foot. He had learned how to survive on only wild game and a bag of corn. It was a dangerous, difficult trip, but he made it.

In Montreal, he loaded another boat with supplies and sailed back toward Fort Crèvecoeur. On the way, however, he learned some horrible news. The soldiers at the fort had rebelled. They had driven Tonty off into the wilderness. Now they were traveling around Lake Ontario, looking for La Salle. They thought the journey was a foolish disaster. They wanted to murder La Salle.

La Salle was furious. He sailed at once into Lake

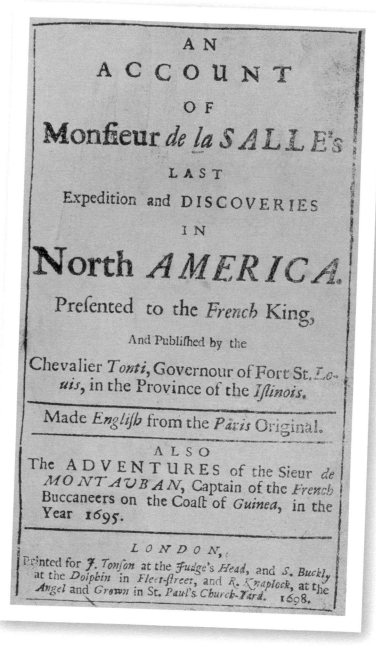

AN
ACCOUNT
OF
Monſieur *de la* SALLE's
LAST
Expedition and DISCOVERIES
IN
North AMERICA.
Preſented to the *French* King,
And Publiſhed by the
Chevalier *Tonti*, Governour of Fort St. *Lo-uis*, in the Province of the *Iſlinois*.

Made *Engliſh* from the *Paris* Original.

ALSO
The ADVENTURES of the Sieur *de MONTAUBAN*, Captain of the *French* Buccaneers on the Coaſt of *Guinea*, in the Year 1695.

LONDON,
Printed for *J. Tonſon* at the *Judge's Head*, and *S. Buckly* at the *Dolphin* in *Fleet-ſtreet*, and *R. Knaplock*, at the *Angel* and *Crown* in St. Paul's Church-Yard. 1698.

Henri de Tonty wrote about his explorations with La Salle.

Michilimackinac overlooks the Straits of Mackinac. The site of a French fort built in the early 18th century is now a state park.

Ontario. He quickly captured the soldiers and sent them back to Montreal in chains.

But where was his friend Tonty? La Salle searched the waters and forests around Fort Crèvecoeur, but Tonty was nowhere to be found. In fact, he had been wounded in an Iroquois attack and had fled to the north. After an entire year, La Salle finally found his old friend. He was at a settlement called Michilimackinac, on the Straits of Mackinac, where Lake Huron joins Lake Michigan. By the autumn of 1681, La Salle felt he had wasted enough time. He wanted to explore the Mississippi.

Laying Claim to Louisiana

La Salle and Tonty got a few canoes together. Then, along with some Frenchmen, Indians, and a priest, they entered the Illinois River. It led them directly to the Mississippi River, just north of what is now St. Louis, Missouri.

In February 1682, La Salle began traveling down the river

La Salle and his party are shown entering the Mississippi River in canoes in February 1682 in this painting by American artist George Catlin.

IN · HONOR · OF ·
RÉNÉ·ROBERT·CAVALIER·SIEUR·DE·LA·SALLE
& HENRY · DE · TONTI ·

A bronze plaque on the North Michigan Avenue bridge
of the Chicago River honors La Salle and Tonty.

toward the Gulf of Mexico. On the first day, the explorers passed the mouth of the great Missouri River. A few days later, they saw the Ohio River enter the Mississippi from the east. Once they passed the mouth of the Arkansas River, they had gone farther than any European explorer had before. Spring was in the air as they canoed past lush pine forests and pleasant meadows.

Finally, the river branched out into a wide delta—a fan-shaped cluster of streams. The mighty river was opening up to meet the Gulf of Mexico. On April 9, 1682, La Salle gazed upon a sea of blue stretching as far as he could see. He had reached the river's end.

Dressed in a gold-laced red cloak, La Salle went ashore near present-day Venice, Louisiana. He put up a cross and a stone marker with King Louis's name. Then he claimed the river and all the land whose waters fed into it for France. He named this vast region *Louisiana*, in honor of King Louis XIV.

At the time, La Salle had no idea how huge this region was. Some of the longest rivers in

La Salle and his companions on the Mississippi River

La Salle claimed a huge territory in North America for France and named it Louisiana.

North America flow into the Mississippi. The Missouri River, for example, starts high in the Rocky Mountains and flows through present-day Montana, North Dakota, and South Dakota. Then it passes along the borders of Nebraska, Iowa, Kansas, and Missouri. Finally, it crosses Missouri before emptying into the Mississippi River.

All La Salle knew was that he had done a great favor for the king of France. Now it was time to collect his reward.

La Salle claimed all waters flowing into the Mississippi, including the huge Missouri River, shown in this nineteenth-century painting by Karl Bodmer.

The Death of a Dream

Soon La Salle was back in France. King Louis welcomed the news of the land La Salle had claimed for France. At once, La Salle began to argue his case for a colony. He was so set on his plan that he began bending the truth.

At this time, Spain owned a colony in the Americas, too. It was called New Spain. Its capital was in Mexico City, but it went as far north as present-day Texas, California, New Mexico, Arizona, and beyond. New Spain's great river was the

King Louis XIV

Rio Grande. Today the Rio Grande forms the border between Texas and Mexico. Like the Mississippi, it empties into the Gulf of Mexico.

La Salle lied about the exact location of the mouth of the Mississippi. He told the king that it was much farther west than it really is. Surely we must build a colony at the mouth of the Mississippi, he said. Then France would be in a great position to fight New Spain. The more he talked, the more he lied. Eventually he said that the Mississippi and the Rio Grande were one and the same river!

King Louis listened. His desire to take over New Spain

The port of La Rochelle is shown in an early twentieth-century
painting by famous French artist Paul Signac.

clouded his good sense. He agreed that La Salle should make a colony in Louisiana. He gave La Salle four ships, along with soldiers, craftsmen, and settlers for the new colony.

On July 24, 1684, La Salle and the settlers set sail from the French port of La Rochelle. In February 1685, they pulled into present-day Matagorda Bay, on the Gulf Coast of Texas. Matagorda Bay is about halfway between the mouth of the Mississippi and the mouth of the Rio Grande. At that point, a river called the Rio Bravo flows into the Gulf of Mexico. La Salle claimed that they had reached the mouth of the Mississippi—or, as

French artist Theodore Gudin painted this image in 1844 of La Salle's ships landing in Matagorda Bay in what is now Texas.

La Salle's ships in Matagorda Bay were hundreds of miles away from the mouth of the Mississippi River.

he was now saying, one of its many mouths! Some of the French officers argued with him, but La Salle stood firm.

Things went downhill from there. La Salle's supply ship, *Belle*, was wrecked in a storm. Another ship ran aground and sank in the

Top: The excavation of the Belle, *which sank in Matagorda Bay*
Bottom: Researchers sculpted a face to show what a French sailor might have looked like. The sailor's skeleton was found in the sunken Belle.

bay. A third ship headed back for France. Swarms of mosquitoes hung in the hot, muggy air, feasting on the miserable crew. The men became weak with fever and disease. Many died. Then the Indians in the area attacked. With no supplies, La Salle decided his only hope was to march overland to Canada. By this time, most of his men hated La Salle. No one wanted to go anywhere with him—and certainly not to the other side of North America!

La Salle picked twenty men for his journey, and they set out for the north. Everyone was angry, and the men's hatred for La Salle grew day by day. By March 19, 1687, a couple of the men had hatched a plan. They hid in some tall grass and waited for La Salle to pass by. Then they sprang out and shot him in the head. La Salle's great dream of his Louisiana empire would never come true.

After La Salle was murdered, the rest of the men wandered around, not knowing where to go. Only seven of them survived. Meanwhile, La Salle's body lay somewhere in Texas. It has never been found.

In the years to come, France and Britain were often at war. Their fighting in Europe spilled over into their North American colonies. By 1760, Britain had won all of Canada and the French settlements on the Great Lakes. In 1763, Britain took control of all French territory east of the Mississippi River.

La Salle was murdered by his own men on March 19, 1687.

The history of New France came to an end in 1803. That year the United States bought the Louisiana Territory from France for about $15 million. This is known as the Louisiana Purchase. The Louisiana Territory stretched from the Mississippi River west to

La Salle was killed near the Trinity River in what is now Texas.

the Rocky Mountains. It doubled the size of the United States.

As for La Salle, only a few men had stayed faithful to him to the end. One was Henri Joutel, who came from La Salle's own hometown of Rouen. Joutel said La Salle had many "fine qualities." But he also had a "haughtiness . . . and a harshness towards those under his command," which caused them to hate him. This, Joutel thought, "was at last the cause of his death." Henri de Tonty, however, saw La Salle with the eyes of a friend. He called the explorer "one of the greatest men of his age."

A large statue of La Salle stands in Luneville, France.

Glossary

colony a territory settled by people from another country and controlled by that country

empire a group of countries that have the same ruler

estate a large piece of property

inherit to be given someone's property after they die

novice a person in training to become a priest

rapids part of a river where water flows very fast

Did You Know?

- La Salle brought thousands of beads, brass rings, and wooden combs to trade in the proposed new colony.

- La Salle's cannons weighed over 800 pounds (360 kilograms), were nearly 6 feet (2 meters) long, and used 4-pound (1.8 kg) iron balls as ammunition.

- La Salle's men used ceramic firepots, similar to modern grenades, to attack and burn wooden enemy ships.

- In 1995, La Salle's wrecked supply ship, *Belle*, was discovered at the bottom of Matagorda Bay, Texas.

- King Louis Philippe of France commissioned famous American artist George Catlin in 1847 to do a series of paintings about La Salle's explorations.

Important Dates in La Salle's Life

1643
La Salle born in Rouen, France

1666
La Salle sails to New France

1669–1671
La Salle explores the Great Lakes and the Midwest

1682
La Salle explores the Mississippi River south to the Gulf of Mexico and claims the Mississippi River Valley

1684
La Salle starts a settlement near the mouth of the Mississippi

1687
La Salle killed by his own men in Texas

Important People

LOUIS DE FRONTENAC (1622–1698) governor of New France

LOUIS JOLLIET (1645–1700) French-Canadian who explored the upper Mississippi River with Father Jacques Marquette in 1673

LOUIS THE FOURTEENTH (LOUIS XIV) (1638–1715) king of France, called the Sun King

JACQUES MARQUETTE (1637–1675) priest who explored the upper Mississippi River with Louis Jolliet in 1673

HENRI DE TONTY (1650?–1704) Italian-born explorer who joined La Salle on his explorations

Want to Know More?

At the Library

Bergen, Lara Rice. *The Travels of Sieur de La Salle*. Austin, Tex.: Raintree/Steck-Vaughn, 2000.

Harmon, Daniel. *La Salle and the Exploration of the Mississippi.* Broomall, Penn.: Chelsea House, 2000.

Nardo, Don. *Sieur de La Salle.* New York: Franklin Watts, 2001.

On the Web

La Salle Shipwreck Project
http://www.thc.state.tx.us/belle/index.html
Describes the exciting discovery of La Salle's wrecked ship *Belle*, with links to sites about La Salle and his explorations

Through the Mail

Mariners' Museum
100 Museum Drive
Newport News, VA 23606
757/596-2222
800/581-7245
Museum on the Age of Exploration, with exhibits of ships and maritime artifacts. Free museum brochure on request.

On the Road

Mississippi River Museum
P.O. Box 266
Third Street Ice Harbor
Dubuque, IA 52004-0266
319/557-9545
800/226-3369
Explores more than 300 years of Mississippi River history, with historic watercraft, Native American artifacts, a National Rivers Hall of Fame, and a walk below the river's surface

Index

About the Author

Ann Heinrichs grew up in Fort Smith, Arkansas. She began playing the
piano at age three and thought she would grow up to be a pianist.
Instead, she became a writer. Now she has written more than fifty
books for children and young adults. Several of her books have won
national awards. Ms. Heinrichs now lives in Chicago, Illinois. She
enjoys martial arts and traveling to faraway countries.